Black Achievement IN SCIENCE

Chemistry

MC

Mason Crest

Black
Achievement
IN SCIENCE

Biology

Chemistry

Computer Science

Engineering

Environmental Science

Inventors

Medicine

Physics

Space

Technology

Black
Achievement
IN SCIENCE

Chemistry

By JANE GARDNER
Foreword by Malinda Gilmore and Mel Poulson,
National Organization for the Advancement of
Black Chemists and Chemical Engineers

Mason Crest
450 Parkway Drive, Suite D
Broomall, PA 19008
www.masoncrest.com

© 2017 by Mason Crest, an imprint of National Highlights, Inc.

Printed and bound in the United States of America.

Series ISBN: 978-1-4222-3554-6
Hardback ISBN: 978-1-4222-3556-0
EBook ISBN: 978-1-4222-8323-3

First printing
1 3 5 7 9 8 6 4 2

Produced by Shoreline Publishing Group LLC
Santa Barbara, California
Editorial Director: James Buckley Jr.
Designer: Patty Kelley
Production: Sandy Gordon
www.shorelinepublishing.com

Cover photographs by Photosky/Dreamstime.com.

Library of Congress Cataloging-in-Publication Data on file with the Publisher.

Contents

Key Icons to Look for

Words to Understand: These words with their easy-to-understand definitions will increase the reader's understanding of the text, while building vocabulary skills.

Research Projects: Readers are pointed toward areas of further inquiry connected to each chapter. Suggestions are provided for projects that encourage deeper research and analysis.

Text-Dependent Questions: These questions send the reader back to the text for more careful attention to the evidence presented here.

Series Glossary of Key Terms: This back-of-the-book glossary contains terminology used throughout this series. Words found here increase the reader's ability to read and comprehend higher-level books and articles in this field.

Educational Videos: Readers can view videos by scanning our QR codes, providing them with additional educational content to supplement the text. Examples include news coverage, moments in history, speeches, iconic moments, and much more!

cience, Technology, Engineering and Mathematics (STEM) are vital to our future, the future of our country, the future of our regions, and the future of our children. STEM is everywhere and it shapes our everyday experiences. Science and technology have become the leading foundation of global development. Both subjects continue to improve the quality of life as new findings, inventions, and creations emerge from the basis of science. A career in a STEM discipline is a fantastic choice and one that should be explored by many.

In today's society, STEM is becoming more diverse and even internationalized. However, the shortage of African Americans and other minorities, including women, still exists. This series—***Black Achievement in Science***—reveals the numerous career choices and pathways that great African-American scientists, technologists, engineers, and mathematicians have pursued to become successful in a STEM discipline. The purpose of this series of books is to inspire, motivate, encourage, and educate people about the numerous career choices and pathways in STEM. We applaud the authors for sharing the experiences of our forefathers and foremothers and ultimately increasing the number of people of color in STEM and, more

By Malinda Gilmore, NOBCChE Executive Board Chair and Mel Poulson, NOBCChE Executive Board Vice-Chair

specifically, increasing the number of African Americans to pursue careers in STEM.

The personal experiences and accomplishments shared within are truly inspiring and gratifying. It is our hope that by reading about the lives and careers of these great scientists, technologists, engineers, and mathematicians, the reader might become inspired and totally committed to pursue a career in a STEM discipline and say to themselves, "If they were able to do it, then I am definitely able to do it, and this, too, can be me." Hopefully, the reader will realize that these great accomplishments didn't come easily. It was because of hard work, perseverance, and determination that these chosen individuals were so successful.

As Executive Board Members of The National Organization for the Professional Advancement of Black Chemists and Chemical Engineers (NOBCChE) we are excited about this series. For more than 40 years, NOBCChE has promoted the STEM fields and its mission is to build an eminent cadre of people of color in STEM. Our mission is in line with the overall purpose of this series and we are indeed committed to inspiring our youth to explore and contribute to our country's future in science, technology, engineering, and mathematics.

We encourage all readers to enjoy the series in its entirety and identify with a personal story that resonates well with you. Learn more about that person and their career pathway, and you can be just like them.

**W**hen you think about chemistry class do you picture yourself in a lab coat, hunched over a beaker of bubbling liquid? Or do you see tables and charts and calculations with arrows and numbers, subscripts and superscripts? Those are all things that students of chemistry, and actual chemists, do in their careers. But the study of chemistry and the role chemistry plays in our lives is so much more than lab work and formulas.

Chemistry is the study of everything about matter— from its composition, to its structure, to its properties, and

Using lab equipment like this, chemists can study just about everything in the world that is made of matter.

how it reacts with other things. Chemistry is all around you. Consider this. Did you make toast this morning for breakfast? Fry an egg in a pan? Wash your hair with shampoo? Take a vitamin? Add bleach to a load of laundry? Or ride in an automobile? All of these things happened because of chemistry, chemical reactions, and interactions of different types of matter.

Chemists study chemicals. Chemicals always have the same composition and the same properties, no matter where they are found. Chemicals make up everything around you. And chemists work with chemicals and their properties in different settings. Some chemists may work in a lab to come up with new ways to keep our foods safe. Environmental chemists collect water samples from contaminated streams and devise ways to clean them up. Medical chemists work with medicine to come up with new cures for diseases, new vaccinations, and new drug treatments. Hazmat chemists protect us from hazardous waste and radioactivity. Forensic chemists help to solve crimes with sophisticated technology. Chemists work in laboratories, conducting experiments, and analyzing data. And chemists even interpret data from outer space, expanding our knowledge of the chemicals that shape the worlds far beyond our own.

This book is part of a series highlighting the achievements of black scientists. As you will read, many of the black chemists in this book were met with opposition and prejudice. The chemists introduced here range from George Washington Carver, who was born into slavery in the 1800s, to Willie E. May who heads the National Institute of Standards and Technology. Even the more modern-day chemists met with opposition. These scientists have arrived to job interviews only to be told that they should be applying for the position of janitor, or given the task of doing simple math, rather than the sophisticated science they were trained to do. Not only are these scientists notable for their scientific and educational accomplishments, but also for the social and personal obstacles they overcame in their pursuit of education and science.

The chemists featured in this book came from all over the US and the world. Some gave back to society by discovering important treatments for disease, or by leading government agencies to improve everyone's health, or by inspiring groups of African-American elementary students to pursue careers in science or engineering. Others became teachers, passing their love of science on to generations of students. Others looked beyond the borders of the US, working to establish schools and access to education in remote African villages. These chemists were, and are, more than simply

Pursuing a career in chemistry will start with learning how to work in a lab.

Chemists learn symbols and a system of diagrams that help them explain chemical elements and bonds.

scientists in lab coats. They are examples of how science can help others.

There are countless chemists, scientists of all races, who have done amazing things and overcome obstacles along the way. This is the story of only eight of these chemists. But, perhaps you will be inspired by their strength and determination and use their model as a model for part of your own life. ●

Words to Understand

botany
the study of plant biology

chemurgy
use of food products for nonfood uses

pathology
the study of diseases and the changes they cause in organisms

Chapter 1

George Washington Carver

Born:
1864(?)

Died:
1943

Nationality:
American

Achievements:
Pioneered multiple uses of crops such as the peanut; inventor, educator, botanist, chemist.

T he exact date of George Washington Carver's birth is uncertain. He was born a slave in Mississippi sometime around 1864. This was toward the end of the American Civil War and Carver's mother, Mary, was owned by Mr. Moses Carver. Carver's father was a slave owned by a neighbor, but he was killed in an accident before Carver was born. Carver and his mother were kidnapped when he was a baby. Their owner, Mr. Carver, hired someone to find Mary and her baby. Mary died under suspicious circumstances and only baby George was returned to the Carver home.

With the end of the Civil War and slavery in 1865, young Carver had a new home. Moses Carver and his wife, Susan, took him in and raised him. He was sickly as a young boy, and was not much help in the fields or

on the farm. He spent most of his time helping with household chores such as cooking, laundry, and sewing.

The Carvers taught George to read and write. As a result, he gained an appreciation for learning and a thirst for knowledge. George left the Carver home when he was young to go to a school for black children. Eventually, after attending several different schools, he graduated from Minneapolis High School in Kansas. He was accepted to Highland College but when he arrived on campus, he was asked to leave. The administrators did not realize he was black, and indicated that they did not accept students of his race. Several years later, he applied and was accepted to Iowa State Agricultural College in Ames.

Carver was interested in many things: music, art, botany, chemistry, and agriculture. He eventually decided to study **botany** and went on to earn both a bachelor of science degree and a master's degree in plant **pathology** at Iowa State.

He wanted to take his knowledge of botany and share it with other students as a teacher and a researcher. In 1896, he was hired by Booker T. Washington to run the agricultural department at Tuskegee Institute in Alabama. Tuskegee, a school for blacks only, was founded in 1881 as part of the effort to expand education for blacks after the Civil War. George Washington Carver enjoyed special status at Tuskegee. He had received much attention for his research and studies and was one of the only faculty members with a degree from a school that typically did not admit black students.

Thrasher Hall is one of several buildings still in use at Tuskegee from the time of Carver's work there.

Carver is probably most well known for his work with the peanut. The peanut was a good plant to work with for several reasons. First, the peanut is very easy to grow. It also helps enrich the soil as it grows, replacing vital nutrients in the soil that other plants need to grow. And the peanut is also a very good source of protein. This was important because many of the farmers that George was working with at the time were poor black farmers who could not afford to add much meat to their diets.

Carver's work with the peanut and its chemical and biological properties led to the development of many new products including milk, butter, cooling oils, Worcestershire sauce, face creams, and hand lotions. In fact, he came up with more than 300 new products from the peanut—food, industrial, and commercial products.

His approach to using a plant, like the peanut, for things other than food products is called **chemurgy**. Chemurgy is a term used by scientists and people in industry to explain

the method by which nonfood uses were found for food products.

Carver spent much of his career as a researcher working with the ideas surrounding chemurgy in his mind. In particular, he found that planting legumes in a field could increase the nutritional content of the soil. Legumes include plants such as alfalfa, peas, soybeans, lentils, and peanuts. Legumes contain bacteria in their roots that have a special ability to take nitrogen from the atmosphere and turn it

By understanding the chemistry of how plants grow, Carver was able to help farmers increase the yield of their crops.

into a form of nitrogen that is needed as a nutrient in soil. The idea of taking a plant and using it to increase the fertility of the soil without the use of expensive fertilizers was one of the foundations of Carver's research.

George Washington Carver was an inventor, an educator, and a scientist. Many of the advances he made in the area of agriculture directly improved the lives and livelihood of black farmers who were struggling to make ends meet. He sought to improve the lives of others—and accomplished that goal! ●

This 1998 stamp honoring Carver was actually the second issue; the first was a 3-cent stamp in 1948.

George Washington Carver: Accomplished man of science

Words to Understand

daguerreotype
a photographic process by which a sheet of copper is polished until it is very shiny; it is exposed to fumes that make it sensitive to light and then exposed to various amounts of light in a camera

Hansen's disease
also known as leprosy, a highly contagious disease that causes skin sores, muscle weakness, and paralysis

pharmaceutical chemistry
branch of chemistry that focuses on finding new treatments and medicines

Chapter 2

Alice Ball

Born:
1892

Died:
1916

Nationality:
American

Achievements:
Found method for treating
leprosy still being used today

Alice Ball lived a life of firsts—first woman and first African American to graduate from the University of Hawaii with a master's degree and the first female chemistry professor. These are significant accomplishments. And they are even more significant if you consider the fact that Alice Ball died tragically young at the age of 24. Imagine what else she could have accomplished.

Alice Ball was born in 1892 in Seattle, Washington. Science, and in particular chemistry, already played an important role in her family. Her grandfather, JP Ball, was a well-known photographer. He was known for his **daguerreotype** photographs. One of the most commonly used methods of photography at the time, daguerreotype was a photographic process by which a sheet of copper is polished until it is very shiny. It is exposed to

fumes that make it sensitive to light and then exposed to various amounts of light in a camera. It is then treated with chemicals and dried. This was sophisticated photography at the time, and the use of chemicals made it a complicated process that not all photographers were successful with. Ball's grandfather was accomplished at the technique, and perhaps her exposure to the processes and chemicals instilled an interest in chemistry in her as a young child.

Ball's family moved to Hawaii and then back to Seattle where she graduated from the University of Washington in 1912. She held a double major there in **pharmaceutical chemistry** and pharmacy. In 1914, she moved back to Hawaii to study at the College of Hawaii (which later became the University of Hawaii). She graduated in 1915 with a master's of science degree in chemistry. After graduation, Ball was the first woman to be offered a position as a chemistry teacher at the University of Hawaii.

Ball's research at the University of Hawaii focused on finding a treatment for people suffering from **Hansen's disease**, which is more commonly known as leprosy. It is caused by bacteria and is highly contagious and debilitating. In the early 1900s, many people feared this disease. People suffering from leprosy have

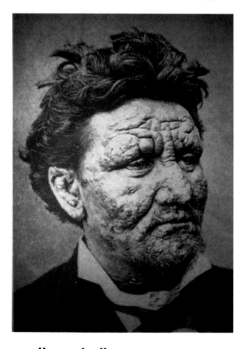

Hansen's disease can cause disfiguring lumps on the skin.

symptoms such as skin lesions, discoloring and growths on the skin, numbness, muscle weakness, paralysis, and severe pain. Patients with leprosy were referred to as lepers. They were often segregated from society in areas known as leper colonies that were far from others people. In fact, there was

a leper colony on the Hawaiian island of Molokai, which was remote and very inaccessible while at the same time very beautiful. In the late 1800s, the number of people with leprosy was increasing rapidly and the government felt that the only way to protect others was to separate those with the disease from the general population. At the time there was no treatment or cure for the disease and it spread very quickly.

The Hawaiian island of Molokai was set up as a way to keep those suffering from Hansen's separate from other people.

Ball's research focused on using chaulmoogra oil to treat the leprosy patients. Chaulmoogra is an herb whose seeds are used in many Asian cultures to treat skin conditions.

Ball found that the oil from the chaulmoogra plant could be injected into leprosy patients and provide some relief.

Prior to Ball's research, chaulmoogra was used in the powder or ointment form to treat skin conditions, such as psoriasis and eczema. Chaulmoogra had been used, with limited success, to help leprosy patients before. The patients had to take the oil orally, and complained of the taste and upset stomachs. Ball was working on a way to inject chaulmoogra into Hansen's disease patients. Her research was successful but she was not immediately given credit for her research. Unfortunately, the success of her research was not without a heavy cost. Ball became ill—some say she fell ill because she was so focused on her research. She returned to Seattle but soon passed away at the age of 24.

The president of the University of Hawaii, Arthur L. Dean, continued Ball's research and published the findings. He did not give Ball credit for her work, and termed the process of injecting chaulmoogra oil as the "Dean Method." Ball's professor and mentor, Harry T. Hollmann complained and got Ball the credit she deserved. The process was renamed the "Ball Method" and as recently as 1999 was still being used to treat patients of leprosy in remote regions of the world ●

Alice Ball:
Hero to Hansen's sufferers

Words to Understand

anesthetics
substances that reduce the amount of pain someone feels

patent
a set of exclusive rights granted to an inventor for a limited period of time in exchange for detailed public disclosure of an invention

sterilize
to destroy microorganisms on an object, usually by heating it to a high temperature with steam, dry heat, or a boiling liquid

Chapter 3

Lloyd A. Hall

Born:
1894

Died:
1971

Nationality:
American

Achievements:
Studied ways to preserve
food without refrigeration;
created inventions that
earned more than 50 patents.

H ave you had a sandwich that contained some sort of deli meat? Have you or a family member had a medical procedure in which medical equipment was **sterilized**? If you answered yes to either of these questions then you have Lloyd A. Hall to thank.

Lloyd A. Hall was an African-American food chemist. He was born in Illinois in 1894, a time when more and more opportunities were opening up for African Americans in the United States, but it was still a time when racism and discrimination were common.

Hall was a standout student and athlete at his high school in Aurora, Illinois. He played baseball, track, and football in high school while also serving as captain of the debate team and earning honors in his class. He was offered four scholarships to college and chose to go to Northwestern University,

in Evanston, Illinois, where he received a bachelor's degree in pharmaceutical chemistry.

Pharmaceutical chemistry is a branch of chemistry that focuses on the development of compounds that can be used as drugs or medicines. At the time of Hall's graduation in 1916, much of the research in the field of pharmaceutical chemistry centered on finding new compounds to create medicines that could be used as **anesthetics** or painkillers.

Hall continued his education after graduation and received a graduate degree in pharmaceutical chemistry from the University of Chicago. He was quickly hired by the Western Electric Company after interviewing with them on the telephone. However, when he arrived at the office for his first day of work, they told him he couldn't work there because they didn't employ black people.

Hall didn't let the racist attitudes at the Western Electric Company hold him back. He soon found a job as a chemist with the Chicago Department of Health and was promoted to the position of senior chemist in a year. A year later, he moved to Iowa for a position as chief chemist at the John Morrel Company, which specialized in cured meats such as ham, bacon, and sausage.

After World War I, Hall married Myrrhene Newsome and the couple eventually moved back to Chicago, where he was employed as chief chemist at a laboratory. There he was able to focus on food chemistry and sought to find a way to preserve meat with chemicals. At the time, many meats were preserved with the addition of salt. Lloyd's

Starting with traditional preservation methods such as spices, Hall found that more advanced techniques worked better.

work focused on adding substances like corn sugar or glycerin as a way to prevent the powder used to preserve meats from forming lumps. He applied for and received many **patents** as a result of his research.

Some of his research looked into the use of spices to preserve food. Many spices could be used to prevent the growth of microorganisms in food. But, as Hall and his colleagues found, some spices also contained bacteria, yeast, or mold spores. This led to a patent to sterilize the spices. The patent was for a method by which the spices were exposed to ethylene oxide gas. The practice was soon abandoned when it was determined that ethylene oxide was actually quite toxic and could cause cancer. Hall and a colleague later helped push for the use of ethylene oxide to sterilize medical equipment.

By the end of his career, Hall had received more than 50 patents in the US and in several other countries. His contributions to the study of food chemistry are indisputable. ●

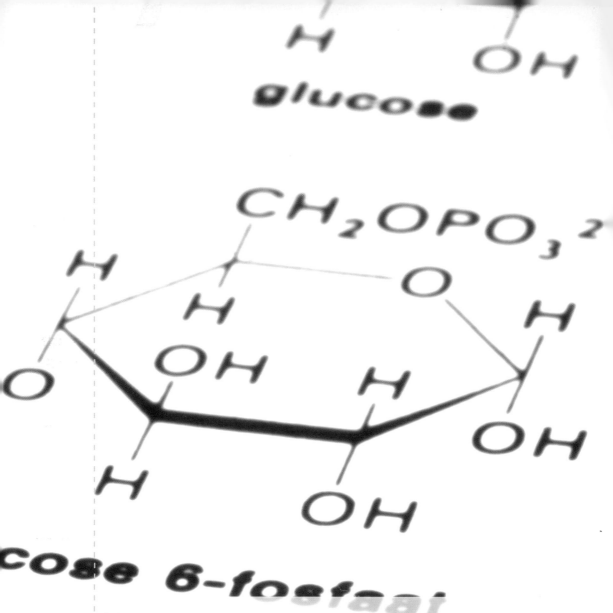

glucose

$CH_2OPO_3^{2-}$

cose 6-fosfaat

Words to Understand

jute fiber
long, soft, vegetable fiber that can be spun into thread

okra
a flowering plant with edible green pods grown in warm climates

organic chemistry
study of the structure and properties of compounds and materials that contain carbon

Chapter 4

Henry McBay

Born:
1914

Died:
1995

Nationality:
American

Achievements:
Award-winning chemist
studied uses of plants,
innovations in plastics and
combustible materials

Henry McBay was born in Mexia, Texas, in 1914. His parents did not have a high school education, primarily because at that time there were no schools open to African Americans in their area. However, after oil was discovered in Mexia, more money and opportunity was brought to the community. One such opportunity was a high school for African-American students. McBay attended this high school and proved to be a strong student, especially in math. As a result, he was encouraged to continue his education and attend college. He was accepted at Wiley College in Marshall, Texas and, because of the influence of several of his high school teachers, chose to study **organic chemistry**.

He was a hard worker and proved this as he studied at Wiley College. He worked at the dining hall and in the college post of-

fice to earn money for his tuition. He finished his bachelor's degree in 1934 and also earned a partial scholarship to graduate school at Atlanta University. McBay got a job at the dining hall there, too, and a few days after he started working there, one of his professors got him a job in a chemistry laboratory where he could use his expertise to work on new projects while earning tuition money.

As part of his job in that lab, McBay worked with a new type of plastic. This new product had properties that were similar to rubber. As a result, McBay began to conduct his

Plastic compounds such as these were the basis for some of McBay's early research; plastic is used in millions of products.

own experiments on plastics as he finished his master's degree.

After graduation, he had a number of different teaching jobs. He went back to teach at Wiley College in part to help his sister and brother pay for college and then taught at a junior college and high school.

After teaching high school math, he took a job at the Tuskegee Institute in Alabama as a chemist. He was part of a team looking for a substitute for **jute fiber**, which was imported from India to make rope and various fabrics in the US. However, shipments of jute were stopped due to World War I.

McBay and his team at Tuskegee hoped that **okra**, a crop grown in Alabama, could be used in place of jute fiber. The team studied okra and discovered that if the plant was allowed to mature, the stems were too brittle to be used as fibers, but if it were harvested before it was mature, then it could not be used as food. McBay's team concluded that okra could be used as food, or as a fiber, but not as both. After this discovery, McBay no longer had a job! The findings did not support further research. Sometimes that happens in science; research and hard work prove that a project is not sustainable.

While at Tuskegee, McBay worked with okra and studied its chemical makeup.

Working with the dangerous but useful hydrogen peroxide, McBay earned a doctoral degree in chemistry.

Eventually, McBay was admitted to the University of Chicago where he began work on a doctoral degree. He worked as a teaching assistant there and developed a first-year chemistry course for undergraduate students.

His research at the University of Chicago focused on highly explosive and dangerous compounds. Specifically, he worked with hydrogen peroxide. Hydrogen peroxide, the liquid often found in a familiar brown bottle in many medicine cabinets, is used at home to sterilize cuts. In the lab, though it can be the basis for many explosive and dangerous chemical reactions. As a result of his research and studies with hydrogen peroxide, McBay earned a doctoral degree in 1945.

He continued his research and his teaching and won several awards, including the Elizabeth Norton Prize for outstanding research in chemistry in 1944 and 1945. He was also given a grant for $5000 to study chemical compounds. Later on, he also served as a technical expert on a UN Educational Scientific and Cultural Organization to Liberia in 1951. The mission was to develop an educational program focused on chemistry for students in the West African nation.

Henry McBay was a chemist and a teacher at heart. He wanted to impart a love of chemistry and science to his students. He ended up teaching for more than 40 years in the Atlanta University system and served as the assistant director of the Program for Research Integration and Support for Matriculation to the Doctorate at Clark Atlanta University. He taught chemistry there until his death in 1995. ●

Henry McBay:
Changed food science

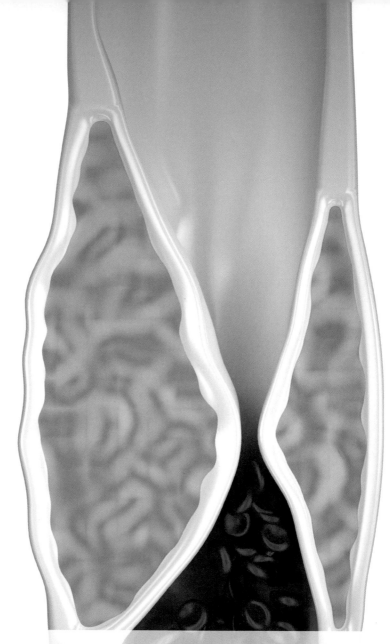

Words to Understand

cholesterol
a vital substance in the body which can become dangerous if levels are too high, leading to an increased risk of heart attacks

protein
large molecules in the body responsible for the structure and function of all the tissues in an organism

Chapter 5

Marie Daly

Born:
1921

Died:
2003

Nationality:
American

Achievements:
Medical chemist who
helped find vital link
between cholesterol
and heart disease

There are many, many applications of chemistry in science, health, and industry. Chemistry plays an important role in medicine as well. Countless chemical reactions occur in our bodies each day, and understanding them can lead to a better understanding of our health, diseases, and how to treat them. Marie Daly used her knowledge and background in chemistry to further understand the human body. This was an important advancement in the world of science and medicine. But she had other lasting impacts on society as well, becoming a role model as one of the first African-American women to earn a doctorate in chemistry. Marie Daly is overcame the obstacles she faced because of her race and gender. Her experiences show how dedication and perseverance can help you achieve any dream.

She was born in 1921 in Queens, New York. Her parents knew the importance of a good education. Her mother, Helen, loved books and would read to young Marie when she was a young child. Her favorite books included those about science and scientists. Her father, Ivan, grew up in the West Indies. In the United States, he enrolled in the chemistry program at Cornell University. This program was too expensive, however, and he moved to New York City to work as a clerk in the post office to support his family.

Daly attended Hunter College High School, an all-girls' school in their neighborhood, where she decided to study chemistry in college. She went to Queens College, and graduated with honors with a bachelor's degree in chemistry in 1942. She went to graduate school at New York University while working part time as a laboratory assistant at Queens College and earned a master's degree in chemistry.

In 1944, she began her doctorate degree at Columbia University. At this time World War II was raging and many of the men who might otherwise work in the sciences were fighting the war. This opened up many opportunities for women at the time.

At Columbia, Daly's research focused on the chemistry of compounds in the body and how some compounds helped with digestion. Three years later, in 1947, her degree was complete and she became the first African-American woman in the United States to earn a PhD in chemistry.

Teaching and research dominated Daly's career as a chemist from that point. She taught at Howard University,

Columbia University, and Albert Einstein College of Medicine at Yeshiva University in New York. She also received grants from the American Cancer Society and The Rockefeller Institute, where she worked on determining how the body's **proteins** are constructed.

Daly's work while at Columbia in New York City has helped save many lives.

Another important research project she worked on at Columbia involved seeking a cause of heart attacks. Daly and her college friend Dr. Quentin B. Deming, found a relationship between high **cholesterol** and clogged arteries. These findings led to a better understanding of the relationship between diet, health, and the circulatory system.

Even with her success as a scientist, researcher, and teacher, Marie Daly never forgot where she came from. She worked hard to develop programs to encourage minority students to attend medical school and graduate-level science programs. She was also instrumental in establishing a scholarship in her fathers' name at Queens College. The scholarship fund was specifically for African-American students interested in pursuing a career in science.

Marie Daly taught biochemistry at the Albert Einstein College of Medicine from 1960 until she retired in 1986. She died in New York City in 2003. ●

accelerator
a device that produces high-energy particles and focuses them on a target

isotope
an atom that has a different number of neutrons in the nucleus than an atom of the same element

periodic table
the arrangement of all the known elements into a table based on increasing atomic number

Chapter 6

James A. Harris

Born:
1932

Died:
2000

Nationality:
American

Achievements:
Part of teams that
discovered new elements;
big advocate of
science careers for
African Americans

Have you ever used the **periodic table** in science class? Even if not, you might still be familiar with it. It is a chart that lists all the known chemical elements and arranges them by their properties. Not often do people think about the fact that someone actually *discovered* all those elements, proved that they exist, and then got to name them. James A. Harris was part of a team that discovered two elements on the periodic table.

James A. Harris was born in Waco, Texas in 1932. His parents divorced while he was still young, and he was raised by his mother. He changed homes often while a young man before moving to California, where he attended high school. He eventually moved back to Austin, Texas, where he attended Huston-Tillotson College. He majored in chemistry there and earned his bachelor's degree in 1953.

Harris joined the US Army and served as a sergeant from 1953 to 1955. After his stint in the army, he began looking for a job as a chemist. He was met with the difficulties and prejudice that faced many African Americans in the 1950s. He would later comment that he could write a book based on his experiences in his job search. He would find that receptionists assumed he was applying for a job as janitor rather than as a chemist. Other hiring managers were shocked when he entered into the interview, surprised to find a well-educated and qualified black man in their office. He persisted, though, and eventually found a job as a chemist at Tracerlab, which was operating as a commercial research lab in Richmond, California.

A few years later, Harris was offered a job at the Lawrence Radiation Lab at the University of California in the Nuclear Chemistry Division. He would spend the rest of his career there. In 1977, he was appointed the head of the Engineering and Technical Services Division at the lab. The Lawrence Berkeley Laboratory was working on finding new elements and completing the periodic table.

Harris worked with a team of scientists as part of the heavy **isotopes** production group, working to create new elements.

Here's a look inside the Lawrence Berkeley Lab.

He would prepare a material by purifying it. The material would then be placed in an **accelerator** and blasted with carbon, nitrogen, and other atoms. This was very difficult and precise work, and Harris was very good at what he did. In 1969, the team bombarded the target element with carbon for hundreds of hours. Then suddenly, for a few seconds, a new element was detected! This element was completely new and was given the number 104; later it was named Rutherfordium. In 1970, that same target element was bombarded with nitrogen, which produced element number 105, later named Hahnium.

Harris did not have a PhD like most of his colleagues at the Lawrence Berkeley Laboratory. He took graduate level courses in chemistry and physics, but spent most of his time in the lab. Houston-Tilloston College gave him an honorary doctorate degree in 1973, in recognition of his work with elements 104 and 105.

Harris recognized the struggle that African-American students, engineers, and scientists faced. He devoted a large amount of his time to recruiting African-American scientists to the lab. He also visited universities, high schools, and elementary schools across the country to encourage African-American students to study science. He was inducted into the Black College Hall of Fame in Atlanta and is included in an exhibit to "Black Pioneers" in the Oakland Museum. He retired from the Berkeley Lab in 1988 and passed away in 2000. ●

Words to Understand

diffusion
movement of atoms or molecules from an area of high concentration to an area of low concentration

liquid chromatography
a laboratory technique in which components of a mixture are separated, identified, and quantified

nanotechnology
manipulation of matter on an atomic or molecular scale

Chapter 7

Willie May

Born:
1946

Nationality:
American

Achievements:
Leading chemist who
has made a life in
government service,
including leading the
National Institute of
Standards and Technology

We all learn hard, but important, lessons when we are children. Willie May grew up in Birmingham, Alabama, in the late 1950s and early 1960s. The lessons he learned there, on the streets of Birmingham and in his own home, provided him with the tools and strength to rise above his neighborhood and the limitations that faced black youth in that time to become the top chemist in the US government.

In a recent interview, May credits much of his success to the people in his life who were looking out for him. People like his parents, who set high expectations for him and his sisters. His parents worked hard and made sacrifices for their children, while expressing to them their expectations that they would rise above their surroundings. Willie was a strong student and an athlete in school.

He also had committed teachers. Some of the few people from his community who went to college became teachers and moved back to teach the neighborhood children. These role models encouraged and challenged May.

He set his sights on Howard University in Washington, DC. This historically black school would offer him many opportunities for the future. He and his friend, Marion Guyton (who later went on to serve as an attorney with the Justice Department), both applied to Howard. Guyton received a full scholarship but May did not hear from the school at all. They had never received his application. He discovered that his high school principal had lost it. To make up for the mistake, the principal arranged for May to receive a scholarship at Knoxville College in Tennessee. Looking back, May realized that this was probably the best option for him. Knoxville College was small, with a diverse student population.

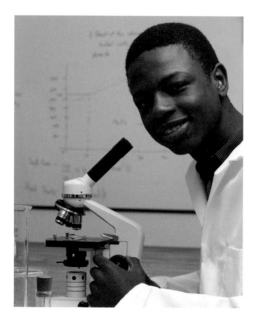

Part of May's work with NIST is to encourage future scientists to follow in his foosteps.

May graduated from Knoxville College with a bachelor's degree in chemistry. He had many options to continue his education in graduate school but accepted a job at the Oak Ridge Gaseous **Diffusion** Plant in Tennessee. After three years there, he was offered a job at

An example of a NIST project: This tiny sensor can be implanted into a patient's brain and send back information to doctors.

the National Bureau of Statistics, now known as the National Institute of Standards and Technology (NIST), which is a government agency in the US Department of Commerce. This agency is made up of scientists, technicians, researchers, and engineers who work to provide specifications and technical requirements for devices used to weigh and measure materials and substances. The NIST is one of the oldest physical science labs in the country. The work done there supports devices from the smallest **nanotechnology** to the largest earthquake-resistant buildings. Scientists at the NIST work in the areas of health, chemistry, bioscience, energy, nanotechnology, math, physics, public safety, and much more.

May's background in chemistry was put to work at the NIST. His research there focused on using and devising standards that could be used to determine the different parts of a mixture. He specifically looked at organic com-

pounds and used techniques such as **liquid chromatography** in his research. His work has led to methods to identify the different organic materials in environmental, food, and other types of samples. This new knowledge has been described and used in many professional papers and has led to more than 250 lectures and talks in the US and around the world.

He continued his education while with the NIST and received a PhD in analytical chemistry from the University of Maryland in 1977.

As the public face of the important government agency, May is often called on to speak at scientific conferences.

Willie May rose through the ranks of the NIST, serving as the principal deputy to the director and became associate director of laboratory programs. He then served as acting director and on May 4, 2015, was confirmed by the US Congress as the Director of the National Institute of Standards and Technology. He continues to head this organization and its labs as they conduct world-class research on countless topics. ●

Willie May:
Scientist and government leader

Words to Understand

segregated
separated, in this case by race

thermodynamics
the study of heat and its relationship with work and energy

Chapter 8

Jennie Patrick

Born:
1949

Nationality:
American

Achievements:
Worked in industry with supercritical fluids; involved in thermodynamics research; leading science educator

Are you curious about the world around you? Do you like to understand how things work and why? Do you dream big and set goals for yourself? As a young child growing up in Alabama, Jennie Patrick would have answered "Yes" to all of those questions. Achieving her goals was not always easy; she came up against a lot of prejudice and racism. But she persevered and became one of the leading research engineers and educators in the field of chemistry. She is an example of how a person can overcome obstacles to reach their goals.

Born in a small town in Alabama in 1949, Jennie Patrick was one of four children. Both her parents only received a sixth-grade education, but they stressed to their children the importance of education and how school could help improve their lives. She was a cu-

rious and imaginative child who loved to read. Her elementary and middle schools were **segregated**. This means that she went to schools that were only for black children. In 1964, she was one of 11 black students who were integrated into Gadsden High School. The school offered more opportunity for Patrick and her fellow black students, including more sophisticated lab equipment and course work. But it was not easy. She had to insist that she be placed in college preparatory classes. Students and teachers alike showed discrimination and prejudice against the black students. In fact, by the time Patrick graduated, half of the black students who started with her had left the school.

Patrick graduated from Gadsden High School with honors and had already decided she wanted to study chemistry. She earned a scholarship to the University of California at Berkeley but chose to stay closer to home and went to Tuskegee Institute in Alabama. She studied chemical engineering there but the program ended while she was there. She transferred to UC Berkeley but her scholarship was no longer valid. She worked while attending Berkeley and was the only woman in the chemical engineering program there. The other students at Berkeley, and some of the faculty members, were racist and told her that she didn't belong there. Patrick didn't let that slow her down, however. She graduated from Berkeley with a bachelor's degree in chemical engineering and would later indicate that the prejudice and challenges she experienced at Berkeley made her stronger and more determined.

Patrick's next move was to the East Coast where she entered into a doctoral program at the Massachusetts Institute of Technology in Cambridge, near Boston. MIT has one of the best engineering programs in the country and there were more black students and professors there as well. She found more acceptance and was met with less prejudice and hostility. She thrived in the competitive and challenging

Patrick was a pioneer at the Massachusetts Institute of Technology, but she found great support from teachers there.

atmosphere at MIT and earned her doctorate in chemical engineering in 1979, becoming the first African-American woman to earn a doctorate in chemical engineering. Her research focused on **thermodynamics** and heat transfer.

After she graduated, Patrick worked as a research engineer. Her first job was with the General Electric Research Laboratory, where she helped develop a program focused on supercritical fluid extraction technology. Supercritical fluid is the term used to describe anything that is at a temperature or pressure where the substance is not a discrete

Like many chemists, Patrick found interesting work in industry, spending time in the General Electric labs working with supercritical fluids.

liquid or gas. Supercritical fluids can move like a gas and dissolve things like a liquid. Patrick and her team used supercritical fluids to separate a substance into its different parts. She worked with that technology for many years as a research manager and assistant to the vice president at another research institution.

Later, Patrick shifted her attention from the research lab to the classroom. She taught as an adjunct professor at Rensselaer Polytechnic Institute and Georgia Institute of Technology in the 1980s. In 1993, she returned to Tuskegee Institute and became the first scientist appointed the Eminent Scholar's Chair. At Tuskegee, she worked to encourage minority students to pursue their education in science and engineering. She founded a mentoring program for girls studying science and helped students develop skills to survive in a hostile environment.

Unfortunately, many of the chemicals she was exposed to for so long in the laboratory impacted her health. When she retired from Tuskegee in 2000, Jennie Patrick helped establish an organization to educate the public on dangers of chemicals in the environment. ●

Chapter 9

Careers in Chemistry

Did any of these stories about chemists inspire you? Are you considering chemistry as a focus for your education in the future? As you have read, there are many different applications of chemistry—from medicine, to research, to the food industry, to the classroom—and there are so many different roles that chemists can play.

One area that chemists spend a lot of focus on today is energy and the environment. Right now, as the population of Earth continues to grow, there is a lot of pressure on sources of food, clean water, and energy. Chemists are working to combat these problems, find new solutions, and to prepare for the future. For example, consider the chemical process of photosynthesis. Plants use the sun's energy to make their own energy. Chemists may work to develop new materials that are able

to capture and use energy in sunlight to expand our food sources. A chemist might work to find ways to improve the efficiency of a power station to enhance our use of natural resources. Many chemists today may work as sustainability consultants, using their knowledge of chemistry to look at carbon footprints or the environmental impact of products we use on a daily basis. Chemistry is not just white lab coats and beakers. It can have a remarkable and exciting impact on our future and the future of the planet.

Are you concerned about health issues? Perhaps chemistry is an avenue you should explore. The world is

Chemists often are called into the field to obtain samples of materials that they can then test and examine back in the lab.

changing at a very rapid place—chemists can help improve human health. Many of the leading cancer researchers in the world have strong backgrounds in chemistry and in particular biochemistry and how our bodies react to the world around them. Modern-day pharmaceutical companies, the makers of the medicines and drugs we use, employ chemists to develop and research their new drugs. Other chemists may do quality control tests on drugs and other active ingredients in medicines. Chemistry and medicine are closely related.

Chemists were involved in everything you find in your medicine cabinet.

Look in your medicine cabinet or under your kitchen sink and you'll see the work of chemists. Many of the cosmetics, lotions, deodorants, and other products we use were made by chemists. Chemists continue to come up with new formulas and new products. They perform tests on the impact that chemicals such as cleaning fluids have on our lives, the lives of our children and our pets. Sometimes chemists work on improving our foods and may even come up with new flavor combinations for products such as chewing gum, candy, or snack foods.

And there are other jobs where a background in chemistry can help you. For example, many government agencies

and corporations have chemists as scientific advisors. Crimes are sometimes solved by forensic evidence, and often chemists are part of the forensic team to analyze biological samples. Other people with a chemistry background may go on to become teachers, writers, or lawyers focusing their efforts on science.

There are so many options for those of you interested in chemistry. If this is you, you can expect to spend a lot of time not only in chemistry, but also in other science and

The study of chemistry translates into a wide range of careers, from education to industry to research and more.

math classes. It is also helpful to have strong writing skills. Chemistry classes usually involve a laboratory component, so if working with chemicals, designing and conducting experiments, and drawing conclusions based on your data sounds like something you are interested in, then you could be on the right path! ●

More ideas to pursue about careers in chemistry

Text-Dependent Questions

1. What do legumes contain that helps to use nitrogen from the air to enrich the soil?

2. Why were patients with leprosy removed from society and isolated?

3. What is the branch of chemistry that focuses on the development of compounds that can be used as medicine?

4. Marie Daly was the first African-American woman to earn what major degree?

5. Name some of the areas in which the National Institute of Standards and Technology works and does research.

6. Name three areas outside of chemistry in which chemists use their skills to create new products or processes.

Suggested Research Projects

Have these stories inspired you? Does the idea of being a chemist interest you? Here are some ideas for topics you could explore in more depth.

1. Like George Washington Carver, see how many nonfood uses you can come up with, both through research and through your own ideas, for foods like popcorn, corn, and peas.

2. James Hall was part of team credited with discovering two elements on the periodic table. The elements his team found, #104 and #105, were the subject of much controversy when they were named. Research the history of the controversy and learn how it was resolved.

3. In 2014, Willie May was appointed the 15th Director of the NIST (National Institute of Standards and Technology). Visit www.nist.gov to find out more about what this government agency does. While there, check out the information about student internships. There might be an opportunity that might interest you.

4. Alice Ball worked to come up with a treatment for patients of Hansen's disease. Learn more about the disease, commonly known as leprosy. The World Health Organization estimates that there are about 180,000 people in the world today suffering from leprosy, most of them in Africa and Asia with about 100 people in the US being diagnosed with the disease. Find out how the disease is spread, what treatments exist for sufferers today, and what is being done to stem outbreaks and the spread of this highly contagious disease.

Find Out More

Websites

www.nobcche.org/
The National Organization for the Professional Advancement of Black Chemists and Chemical Engineers is a great resource. On its website, you will find information for students including programs, events, and job or internship opportunities.

blackinventor.com/
The Black Inventor Online Museum has information and biographies of the top black inventors of the past 300 years!

www.tuskegee.edu/
Learn more about the history of Tuskegee University at its official website.

Books

Benge, Janet and Geoff Benge. *George Washington Carver: From Slaves to Scientists (Heroes of History)*. Seattle, WA: YMAW Publishing, 2011.
Want to read a fascinating biography of a black scientist who overcame slavery to make a big impact on society? Try this book.

Newmark, Ann. *DK Eyewitness Books: Chemistry*. New York, NY: DK Children, 2005.
There is so much to learn about when you study chemistry. Find out more in this book about chemistry!

Sullivan, Otha Richard. *Black Stars: African American Women Scientists and Inventors*. Hoboken, NJ: Wiley, 2009.
Are you interested in finding out more about African-American women scientists? Check out this book.

Series Glossary of Key Terms

botany the study of plant biology

electron a negatively charged particle in an atom

genome all the DNA in an organism, including all the genes

nanometer a measurement of length that is one-billionth of a meter

nanotechnology manipulation of matter on an atomic or molecular scale

patent a set of exclusive rights granted to an inventor for a limited period of time in exchange for detailed public disclosure of an invention

periodic table the arrangement of all the known elements into a table based on increasing atomic number

protein large molecules in the body responsible for the structure and function of all the tissues in an organism

quantum mechanics the scientific principles that describe how matter on a small scale (such as atoms and electrons) behaves

segregated separated, in this case by race

ultraviolet a type of light, usually invisible, that can cause damage to the skin

Index

Photo credits

(Dreamstime.com) Solarseven/DT 8; Anyaivanova/DT 10; AJ Cotton/DT 11; Noam Ammon/DT 12; Homestead National Monument 13; National Park Service 15; Emiralikokal/DT 16; USPS 17; Eugene Kalenkovich/DT 18; University of Hawaii 19; Pierre Arents/Wiki 20; Hoapili/Wiki 21; Wasanajai/Shutterstock 22; Khjrstudio/DT 24; Maksim Pasko/DT 26; Alain Lacroix/DT 28; Xxlphoto/DT 30; Ezumeimages/DT 31; Douglas Mackenzie/DT 32; Decade3d/DT 34; biomagazine.gr 35; Wangkun Jia/DT 37, 51; Maxim Shebeko/DT 38; CPNAS.org 39; Roy Kaltschmidt/Lawrence Berkeley National Laboratory 40; Library of Congress 42; Department of Commerce 43; Ian Allenden/DT 44; Knappe/NIST 45; NIST 46; Ifeelstock/DT 48; HistoryMakers 49; Upstate NYer/Wiki 52; Wavebreakmediamicro/Dollar 54; Patrizio Martorana/DT 56; Steven Cukrov/DT 57; micromonkey/Dollar 58.

About the Author

Jane P. Gardner is the author of more than 30 books for young and young-adult readers on science and other nonfiction topics. She earned a master's degree in geology and a master's degree in education and also has years of experience teaching and developing science curriculum. In addition to writing, Jane also teaches science classes (including chemistry) at North Shore Community College. She lives in Massachusetts with her husband and their two sons.